Invest Like Warren Buffett

Powerful Strategies for Building Wealth

Second Edition

Matthew R. Kratter

www.trader.university

For Paul

Disclaimer

Table of Contents

Your Free Gift

Thanks for purchasing my book!

As a way of showing my appreciation, I've created a "List of 24 Warren Buffett Stocks" for you.

After my book's initial publication, many of my readers asked for help finding the kind of great stocks that we discuss in this book.

So I put together a list of great businesses that are publicly traded. These are the kinds of stocks that Buffett already owns, or would probably own if he were investing smaller amounts of money, or if the price were right.

Download this list of stocks, and add them to your shopping list, so that you will be ready when the stock market sells off.

Simply go here to download your free list:

http://www.trader.university/buffett-bonus

Chapter 1: Why Investing is Easier for You than Warren Buffett

back to top

Warren Buffett is the world's greatest investor. He began his investment career at the age of 11, buying $114 worth of stock. Seventy-three years later, his net worth is almost $70 billion.

How did he do it?

And, more importantly, what can we learn from Buffett's investment strategy that we can use to make money for ourselves?

There are many things that Buffett does that you and I will never be able to imitate. You and I will never purchase an insurance company and invest the float. You and I will never get a phone call from Goldman Sachs, offering us preferred shares with a 10% dividend yield.

On the other hand, the individual investor has many advantages over Buffett. Buffett is currently sitting on over $50 billion in cash that he needs to put to work. Because of the size of this cash pile, Buffett is limited to investing in only the largest companies. And when he buys a stock, he needs to move slowly, to avoid moving the market.

You and I can quickly buy almost any stock, without rumors swirling and moving the price of the stock. We can buy stock in a company of any size, from a micro-cap to a mega cap. We can buy the kind of smaller and faster-growing companies that Buffett was able to buy in his early investing days, but no longer. And we can sell our shares, if and when we choose.

In 1999, Buffett wanted to sell his shares of Coke, which were sporting a lofty average P/E of 47. He was unable to sell for two reasons. One, he was on the board of directors at Coke. Two, his position was too large to be able to make a graceful exit.

You and I will never have these constraints. We are free to learn from the best of Buffett's investment insights, while operating under the radar.

I have studied Warren Buffett and his investments for over 20 years. I have read all of his annual Berkshire letters. Over time, I have tried to distill Buffett's most valuable investing insights.

If I had to summarize Buffett's main investment strategy in one sentence, it would be this:

Buy shares in a few high-quality, well-run businesses at a fair price, and then hold them forever.

Buffett has been preaching and teaching this investment philosophy for the last 40 years. The secret is hidden in plain view. And yet so few investors have put it into practice, even while they have watched Buffett's wealth compound year after year.

The strategy seems too simple to actually work.

Yet, as Buffett reminds us: "There seems to be some perverse human characteristic that likes to make easy things difficult."

And elsewhere: "I don't look to jump over 7-foot bars; I look around for 1-foot bars that I can step over."

In this book, you will learn how to find those 1-foot bars, so that you can step over them, too.

It's not as exciting as jumping over 7-foot bars, but I hope that you will find it even more financially rewarding.

To implement Buffett's investment strategy, you must first learn how to spot a high-quality business (covered in chapters 2, 3, and 4).

Next, in chapter 5, you will learn how much you should pay for a stock.

And finally, in chapter 6, you will learn about some of the best times to buy stocks.

Before we move on, it is important to remember that for Buffett, stocks are not just pieces of paper, or wiggles on a stock chart. Rather, they are ownership interests in real-world businesses that entitle you to a share of the present and future profits of those businesses.

When you purchase a stock, you become a part-owner in that business.

After you purchase a stock, it may move up, or it may move sharply down. Your ownership and your share of the profits and dividends remain, no matter what happens to the stock price.

If the business continues to do well over time (and provided that you paid a reasonable price for your shares), you will make money.

It is now time to learn what constitutes a high-quality business.

Chapter 2: What a Not-So-Great Business Looks Like

back to top

For Buffett, the world is divided into 2 kinds of businesses:

1. Great businesses

2. Everything else

Buffett believes that you should spend most of your time focusing on the former, and ignoring the latter. Time and money are too valuable to waste on researching or investing in a sub-par business.

To understand what constitutes a great business, it might help to first think about what a not-so-great business looks like.

Staples (paper fasteners).

Have you ever thought about the design of the staples in your stapler? Do you have a favorite brand of staples? Do you lay awake at night thinking about when staples 2.0 are going to be released?

Probably not.

When you're at the office supplies store, or on Amazon, you probably buy whatever is available and cheapest.

Staples are a commodity. Lots of different companies make them, but none of those companies really stand out. Have you ever heard of SwingLine, Advantus, PaperPro, Max, or Rapid? I didn't think so.

Manufacturing staples is a price-competitive business. The manufacturer that can produce them at the lowest cost will gain market share. If someone figures out how to make a cheaper staple, the majority of the cost savings will be passed on to the customer.

Staples for paper staplers are made from zinc-plated steel wires that are glued together. The cost of making them is determined by the materials (zinc, steel, glue) and labor (China, Philippines). Whoever can procure the cheapest materials and the cheapest labor will be able to produce the cheapest staples.

I cannot prove it, but I would guess that staples, on an inflation-adjusted basis, have actually gone down in price over time. The price of the raw materials has gone up, but the efficiency of the machines that make them has probably compensated for it (the first staples were probably made by hand).

This is what a not-so-great business looks like. It produces a commodity product in a highly fragmented and competitive marketplace. The company has little to no brand recognition, and no pricing power— any cost savings end up accruing to the customer, rather than to the owner of the business.

Here is a list of industries that contain many price-competitive businesses:

- semiconductor companies

- gas and oil companies

- steel producers

- airlines

- automobile manufacturers

- producers of corn, wheat, rice

- gold, silver, and aluminum mining companies

- gas stations

- restaurants (with a few notable exceptions like McDonalds, Chipotle, etc.)

- textile manufacturers

You can see that most manufacturers tend to be not-so-great businesses. There is a reason that Apple outsources most of its manufacturing, and chooses instead to focus on technology, design, and marketing.

I should mention, of course, that there is nothing wrong with a not-so-great business. They are often great places to work, they provide valuable and necessary goods and services, and the modern economy could not function without them.

However, we are thinking like owners now. We're no longer employees- – we're Scrooge McDuck or Buffett. We want to own only businesses that will maximize our profits over the long term.

It is extremely difficult to become wealthy owning a price-competitive business.

Chapter 3: How to Spot a Great Business

back to top

Now that we have a feel for not-so-great businesses, let's turn to what a great business looks like.

In a 1989 interview, Buffett reveals how he identifies great businesses:

"I look for simple businesses, with consistent performance, and favorable long-term prospects."

Let's take some time to unpack what Buffett is saying.

First, a great business should be simple.

Another way of saying this is that you are able to understand what the business does, and how it makes money. Some businesses that Buffett finds simple (like insurance), you may not. And vice versa-- Buffett rarely invests in tech, but you may find some tech businesses simple to understand.

Before you invest in a company, you need to understand the products or services that it provides. It is even better if you personally use and love the company's products or services. Many people have gotten quite wealthy by buying Apple stock right after they got their first iPhone.

I could never understand exactly what Enron did, which helped me to avoid it as an investment. It is easy to understand what a Coke or Starbucks does.

Second, a great business usually has excellent brand recognition. For example, even my six-year old can identify Apple, Starbucks, Disney, and American Girl (now a subsidiary of Mattel).

Without looking, you might not know the name of the company that makes your stapler or staples. But you immediately recognize Coke, McDonalds, Wrigley, Hershey's, and Colgate, even if you don't personally use their products.

Great businesses occupy a significant slice of consumer mindshare. For example, if someone says "fast food," you probably immediately think of McDonald's, KFC, or Taco Bell. If someone says "running shoes," you think of Nike.

Third, a great business sells products or services that never go out of style, and require very little updating. Fifty years ago, Coke was selling a certain carbonated beverage, and fifty years from now it will still be selling the same carbonated beverage.

Contrast this with a semiconductor company, which must reinvest most of its profits into research and development to produce the next faster chip. Those are profits which will not end up in the investor's pocket.

When you are researching a company, ask yourself if the company was selling the same product 10 years ago, and whether it will be selling the same product 10 years from now.

Fourth, a great business will usually be one where the consumer needs to purchase the product or service again and again.

You probably only buy a new car or a brand-new house a few times in your life. Car manufacturers and homebuilders are usually terrible businesses (Tesla is a discussion for another time and place).

But things like razor blades, fast food, gum, candy, coffee, toothpaste, and soda are being continuously purchased and used up. If they are slightly addictive (candy) to extremely addictive (coffee, cigarettes), so much the better from the business owner's perspective. I will leave each of you to wrestle with any ethical implications. Personally, I would never own a cigarette company, though I would own a coffee company.

Fifth, a great business has pricing power— the power to raise its prices without large numbers of customers defecting. Strong brands make for powerful and profitable businesses because they have pricing power. When I want a Coke, I will buy a Coke. I have no interest in saving ten cents and buying a generic cola. And in ten years from now, I will still be drinking Coke, even though the price will have risen.

Inflation causes prices to rise over time. Because Coke is such a unique product, the company is able to raise its prices right along with inflation, without experiencing any drop-off in sales. Airlines, farmers, and manufacturers are often unable to pass on their increased costs to the consumer.

As Buffett says:

"The single most important decision in evaluating a business is pricing power. If you've got the power to raise prices without losing business to a competitor, you've got a very good business. And if you have to have a prayer session before raising the price by 10 percent, then you've got a terrible business."

(2011 Financial Crisis Inquiry Commission)

Some businesses are able to raise their prices even faster than the rate of inflation. When this happens, it is a gold mine for the owner. After Warren Buffett purchased See's Candies, he realized that the

11

business had untapped pricing power. If your wife loves See's Candies, will you really go to a competitor to buy her a box of Valentine's candy, just because See's price has gone up from $1.95 to $2.25 (as it did in the 1970's)?

Disney has discovered something similar in the last few years. They have massively increased their admission costs at Disneyland, causing sticker shock among parents. But, seriously, how do you say no to your six-year-old? We never pay full price for our airplane tickets, but we always pay full price at Disneyland. Clearly, Disney has pricing power, and you should own it over an airline.

Buffett has come up with a very helpful metaphor that describes what a great business looks like. A great business always has a "moat." Just as a medieval castle used a moat to passively defend itself from its enemies, a great business will have a "durable competitive advantage" or "moat" that protects it from its competitors.

A competitive advantage might include having a strong brand (Coke), having an important patent (like a drug company), being the lowest-cost provider (Walmart, Amazon), or being the only business in town that provides a certain service (doctor, lawyer, bank, quarry).

A "durable" competitive advantage is simply a competitive advantage that is expected to remain for a long time. If your drug patent is about to expire, you do not have a durable competitive advantage. But if your brand is over 100 years old and has significant mindshare (you remember your first Coke as a kid, and now you are introducing your grandson to his first Coke), then its competitive advantage is durable.

A price-competitive business (like a staple manufacturer) has no moat. It is at the mercy of its competitors, and thus must reinvest most of its profits, rather than paying them out to the owner.

To summarize, a great business will have the following characteristics:

1. Simple, easy-to-understand business

2. Strong brand recognition

3. Will be selling the same product or service 10 years from now

4. Consumers need to buy the product or service again and again

5. Able to raise prices with inflation, or even more quickly

In the next chapter, we will examine what the financial statements of a great business look like.

Chapter 4: Sneaky Tricks for Identifying a Great Business from its Financial Statements

back to top

In the previous chapter, we learned what a great business qualitatively looks like. Now it is time to turn to its financial statements.

Financial statements (which include the income statement, the balance sheet, and the statement of cash flows) are the language of business. The more fluent you become in reading them, the better an investor you will be.

If you are a beginner, there is an easy way to get started. I highly recommend the one-page stock analysis provided by Value Line. If you'd like to see free samples of their product for the Dow 30 stocks, you can go here:

https://research.valueline.com/research#list=dow30&sec=list

Click on a company name that you are interested in, and you can download a free pdf.

An even easier way to get the free pdf is to google the company's ticker and the words "value line." So for Coke, you would google: "ko value line." The first search result will be the free pdf.

The nice thing about Value Line is that they provide earnings per share for the last 16 years. This is simply how much money the company made each year, divided by the number of shares of stock that the company had that year.

In addition, Value Line adjusts these earnings to account for nonrecurring gains and losses. If a company loses money on a bad investment in just one year, it should not affect your appraisal of the underlying economic engine of the company.

Let's look at the earnings per share for Coke (all numbers are provided in US dollars):

1999: 0.65

2000: 0.74

2001: 0.80

2002: 0.83

2003: 0.98

2004: 1.03

2005: 1.09

2006: 1.19

2007: 1.29

2008: 1.51

2009: 1.47

2010: 1.75

2011: 1.92

2012: 1.97

2013: 2.08

2014: 2.04

2015: 2.00

Earnings per share fell in 2014 and 2015, but for the most part, you can see a nice smooth uptrend in earnings.

Contrast that with earnings per share from the Ford Motor Company

1999: 5.86

2000: 3.22

2001: – 3.02

2002: 0.15

2003: 0.50

2004: 2.13

2005: 1.25

2006: – 1.50

2007: – 0.19

2008: – 3.13

2009: 0.00

2010: 1.91

2011: 1.95

2012: 1.42

2013: 1.62

2014: 1.16

2015: 1.73

Ford does not have smoothly uptrending earnings like Coke. Rather, earnings bounce around from year to year, and some years even show negative earnings (meaning that Ford lost money that year).

As you can see, Ford is a not-so-great business, and it shows up in the financial statements.

These leads us to our first rule:

A great business will have earnings that show a smooth upward trend.

This is a direct result of its moat and its ability to raise prices consistently. A price-competitive business like Ford must constantly offer special deals on its cars in order to compete. It loses money on many of the cars that it sells (especially during recessions), while Coke never sells its products at a loss.

Now we turn to our second rule:

A great business will show a consistent return on equity (ROE) above 20%.

Return on equity is simply earnings (also known as "net profit") divided by shareholder equity (also known as "book value").

Shareholder equity is simply the total assets of the company minus its total liabilities.

Just as you would figure out your own net worth by adding up all of your assets (house, stocks, cash) and subtracting your debts (mortgage, credit cards), you can figure out a company's "net worth" (or shareholder equity) by adding up its assets and subtracting its debts (also known as "liabilities").

If you own a company that has a net worth of $100 million, would you be happier if it earned $5 million per year, or $20 million?

Clearly the latter.

In the first case, the ROE is 5% ($5 million in earnings divided by shareholder equity of $100 million).

In the second case, the ROE is 20% ($20 million in earnings divided by shareholder equity of $100 million).

A business with a higher ROE is a business that operates more efficiently, or is able to extract more profit from every sale. If the ROE is consistently above 20%, it is very likely that what you are looking at is a great business with a moat.

There is one exception to this rule. Sometimes a company will borrow lots of money (take on debt) in order to boost its ROE. The more money a company borrows, the riskier that company becomes.

We want to distinguish between companies that have high ROE's because they are great businesses, and companies that have high ROE's simply because they are juicing their results with lots of debt.

One way to do this is to follow our third rule:

A great business will show a consistent return on total capital greater than 15%.

Return on total capital (ROTC) is similar to ROE, but also takes into account the amount of long-term debt that a company carries. It is calculated as follows:

(net income + interest expense)/(shareholder equity + long-term debt)

Fortunately, Value Line calculates both ROE and ROTC so that you don't have to.

If you are looking for a free source, try Morningstar:

http://financials.morningstar.com/ratios/r.html?t=KO&region=USA &culture=en_US

Let's first take a look at ROE for Coke:

2005: 31.8%

2006: 32.9%

2007: 27.5%

2008: 34.4%

2009: 27.5%

2010: 26.3%

2011: 28.2%

2012: 27.5%

2013: 28.3%

2014: 30.0%

2015: 34.4%

We can see that Coke has an ROE that is consistently in the high 20's or low 30's. Both the level of ROE and its consistency are impressive.

Now let's turn to the ROE for Ford:

2005: 18.8%

2006: NMF ("no meaningful figure")

2007: NMF

2008: NMF

2009: NMF

2010: NMF

2011: 52.5%

2012: 35.5%

2013: 25.0%

2014: 18.7%

2015: 24.2%

Unlike Coke, Ford's ROE bounces around a lot. For many of the years, the ROE is not calculated ("no meaningful figure") because the earnings were negative (i.e. the company lost money). From 2011-2013, the ROE is at an impressive level, but sharply declining.

Perhaps Ford has become a great business in the last 4 years?

One look at the ROTC for Ford will dispel any thoughts that Ford might be a great business:

2005: 4.5%

2006: 0.5%

2007: NMF

2008: NMF

2009: 3.7%

2010: 16.5%

2011: 13.2%

2012: 7.4%

2013: 8.2%

2014: 6.1%

2015: 5.3%

Here the ROTC is either NMF or far below the level of 15% (except for 2010) that we have required.

Contrast that with the ROTC for Coke:

2005: 29.8%

2006: 30.7%

2007: 24.2%

2008: 30.6%

2009: 23.4%

2010: 18.5%

2011: 20.2%

2012: 19.4%

2013: 18.3%

2014: 18.7%

2015: 16.5%

As required for a great business, the ROTC for Coke is consistently above 15%.

We mentioned earlier that the more debt a company takes on, the riskier it becomes. A little debt might be useful, so how much is too much?

This leads us to our fourth rule:

Buffett typically invests in companies where the long-term debt could be paid off using 4 years or less of net profit.

(One exception to this rule is the banks and insurance companies that Buffett owns, but that is a discussion for another place.)

For example, Coke currently has about $28 billion in long-term debt. Earnings for the last 3 years have averaged $9.09 billion per year. That means that Coke could pay off all of its debt in about 3 years (28/9.09).

Contrast that with Ford. Ford currently has about $129 billion in long-term debt. Earnings for the last 3 years have averaged $6.05 billion per year (of course, as we have seen, Ford's earnings are anything but dependable— next year it could lose massive amounts of money). So it would take Ford 21 years to pay off all of its debts (129/6.05)!

Any way you slice it, Ford is not a great business, while Coke is.

Let us conclude with our fifth rule:

A great business pays a dividend and/or buys back stock.

A young great business is often better off plowing its earnings back into the business, in order to keep growing.

But for the kind of mature, blue-chip companies that we are discussing (and which Buffett invests in), these great businesses will often generate more cash than they need to maintain their market share.

If that cash cannot be reinvested back into the business at a reasonable return, it makes much more sense to return that cash to shareholders (us!) in the form of dividends or stock buybacks (share repurchases).

A dividend is simply a cash payment to shareholders. Most dividends are paid 4 times a year (on a quarterly basis), and are taxed at a lower rate than other income.

Over the last 3 years, Coke has paid a total of $16 billion in dividends to its shareholders.

Stock buybacks are when a company uses its own money buy shares of its own stock. This has the effect of returning cash to shareholders by increasing their ownership in the company (by reducing the number of shares outstanding).

Over the last 3 years, Coke has bought back $8.5 billion of its stock.

Coke is simply an amazing economic engine that churns out mountains of cash. Free cash flow (money that can be taken out of the business, without hurting its prospects) for the last three years has been over $24 billion.

As Charlie Munger (Buffett's business partner at Berkshire Hathaway) is fond of saying:

"We want to own businesses that drown us in cash."

To summarize, a great business will show the following characteristics in its financial statements:

1. Earnings show a smooth upward trend

2. Consistent return on equity (ROE) greater than 20%

3. Consistent return on total capital (ROTC) greater than 15%

4. Long-term debt less than 4 times earnings

5. Pays a dividend and/or buys back stock

Chapter 5: How Much to Pay for a High-Quality Business

back to top

Now that we have learned how to identify a great business (both qualitatively and from its financial statements), we must answer the question:

How much should we pay for a great business?

Let's begin by imagining a black box that consistently spits out $1,000 every year.

How much would you pay to own this black box?

If you paid $100,000 for the black box, and it returned $1,000 to you every year, you would have an investment that has a yield of 1% (1,000/100,000).

Is 1% a good yield?

Well, that depends. Chiefly, it depends on where interest rates are.

Right now, I can open up a 1 year CD or savings account and earn a 1% yield. These accounts are all government-insured, so I would probably see no reason to risk my money on a black box that also pays only 1% and might stop working someday.

What if I pay $10,000 for the black box? In this case, I will have an investment with a yield of 10% (1,000/10,000). Now I am certainly much happier with this yield. It is not something that I can find anywhere else, so I would probably be quite happy owning the black box at this level.

When you purchase a stock, you are buying partial ownership in a black box. This black box also happens to be a public corporation that makes and sells products to the public.

We don't know the secret formula for Coke, but we do know that this particular black box currently spits out roughly $1.95 per share in earnings. Of that, $1.40 gets paid out in dividends and $0.55 is kept by the company ("retained earnings") to grow the business. If Coke does a good job with its retained earnings and invests it at a higher rate than we could personally do, we are happy to let it hold on to the $0.55. It will grow the $0.55 and eventually pay it back to us down the line as dividends.

So how much should we pay for a share of Coke?

As I'm writing this, you can buy a share of Coke for $45.86. If that share spits out $1.95, then my investment has a yield of 1.95/45.86 or 4.25%. This is often referred to as the "earnings yield" of a stock.

You can calculate it in one of 2 ways:

1. Earnings per share divided by the stock's price per share

2. Net profit divided by the market cap

If Coke were a black box, then this investment would always pay me 4.25% every year. This is pretty good, considering that right now, I can only make 1% or less on my cash in a savings account.

But it gets even better. Coke currently pays me $1.95 per share, but if they grow their earnings, this amount will rise.

Coke is little bit like a bond, but with a yield that should grow over time.

You probably already know about earnings yield, but in its inverse form: the P/E, or price-to-earnings ratio. Earning yield (E/P) is simply the inverse of the price-to-earnings ratio (P/E).

The next time you hear the P/E of a stock, try flipping it over, to see what its earnings yield is.

So, for example, a stock with a P/E of 20 has an earnings yield of 5%. A stock with a P/E of 50 has an earnings yield of just 2%. Obviously in the latter case, the market believes that the earnings will grow sharply over time, so that the earnings yield will rise over time. That is something that may or may not happen.

In 1999, Microsoft (MSFT) earned $0.70 per share, sold for an average P/E of 49.8 and traded between $34 and $60 per share. Ten years later, in 2009, it earned $1.63 per share. As expected by the market, the earnings did in fact grow sharply. In the meantime, the price that the market was willing to pay for $1.00 of Microsoft's earnings (i.e. the P/E) went from 49.8 down to 13.4. In 2009, Microsoft never traded above 31.50. Microsoft started with a high P/E, grew its earnings strongly, and yet the stock went nowhere for a decade.

The lesson? Be very wary of paying a high P/E for a stock, even if it is a high quality company.

This makes sense, when you invert the P/E and think about it as an earnings yield. At a P/E of 50, Microsoft had an earnings yield of 2%, which is a pretty good approximation of the annual return (including dividends) that Microsoft had over that lost decade.

So how much should you pay for a mature, slow-growing, high-quality business like Coke?

That depends on what earnings yield you are content with. Personally, I would not pay more than a P/E of 20 (earnings yield of 5%) for a company like Coke.

Coke has been growing its sales (revenues) at about 8% annually over the past 5 years, and its earnings at about 5.5% annually over the same period.

If you find a company that is growing its earnings faster than that, you might be able to justify a higher P/E.

If Coke's earnings today are $1.95/share and it is able to continue to grow them at 5.5% annually, its earnings will be $3.33 in 10 years from now. At a current price of $45.86, that translates to a future earnings yield of 7.26% (3.33/45.86). If Coke grows its earnings to $3.33 and continues to pay out roughly 65% of its earnings as dividend, the dividend in 10 years from now will be $2.16, giving Coke a dividend yield of 4.71% on today's price.

Of course, Coke's growth could be faster or slower over the next decade. Ultimately, this kind of analysis is more art than science. If you have strong beliefs about whether soda consumption in the US and worldwide will increase or decline, you can come up with a reasonable guess as to whether Coke will grow more quickly or more slowly than the 5.5% annual rate that it has averaged over the last 5 years.

If Coke will grow its earnings significantly more quickly than 5.5%, then you might be able to justify paying a P/E of more than 20.

If Coke will grow its earnings significantly more slowly than 5.5%, then perhaps you should pay a P/E of less than 20.

Warren Buffett bought his shares of Coke in 1988 and 1989 at a split-adjusted average price of just $2.45 per share. In 2015, Coke paid $1.32 in dividends. That gives Buffett a dividend yield of 53.88% on his cost. It is no wonder that the man is a billionaire.

The good news is that you can do something like this, too. If you purchase a great business at a good price and hold it for 25 years, the dividend yield on your cost should also be quite high.

Chapter 6: The Best Time to Buy Stocks

back to top

In the previous chapter, we learned how to use the earnings yield of a stock (and its growth rates) to think about how much to pay for a great business.

There is, fortunately, an even easier method to time your purchases of stock.

In the middle of the 2008 financial crisis, Buffett wrote:

"A simple rule dictates my buying: be fearful when others are greedy, and be greedy when others are fearful."

and

"Bad news is an investor's best friend. It lets you buy a slice of America's future at a marked-down price."

The easiest time to buy a great business at a great price is during a bear market.

In 2008, Coke had earnings per share (EPS) of $1.51. In 2009, Coke traded as low as 18.70, on a split-adjusted basis. At that price, Coke had a trailing P/E of just 12.38, an earnings yield of 8.08%, and a dividend yield of 4.39%.

By comparison, today Coke has a P/E of 23.52, an earnings yield of 4.25%, and a dividend yield of 3.05%. The stock has more than doubled from the lows, all while paying a healthy dividend every year.

Anyone could have bought Coke below $20 in 2009, but very few did. It did not require inside information, or stock tips. All that it required was nerves of steel to buy when it appeared that the financial world was ending.

How long into a bear market should one wait to buy a great business?

One method is just to wait for the dividend yield to get to 4%, or the trailing P/E (calculated using the company's last 12 months of earnings) to get to 15 or lower on a stock like Coke. That is the "valuation method."

The second method is the "market timing" method. It involves waiting a fixed period of time into a bear market before buying- – or waiting for a large peak to trough draw down in price.

For example, Coke peaked at 44.47 (split-adjusted) in July 1998. It fell until March 2003, trading as low as 18.50. In other words, it fell roughly 58% from peak to trough.

Again, Coke peaked at 32.79 in January 2008, before the financial crisis really got started. It fell until March 2009, trading as low as 18.72. In other words, it fell roughly 43% from peak to trough.

Using this "market timing" method, you would wait for Coke to sell off 40-50% from its last highest price, and then buy your position.

Since Coke is a blue-chip stock that is included in indices like the Dow Jones Industrial Average and the S&P 500, it tends to bottom at the same time that the general stock market bottoms.

The 2000-2002 bear market lasted roughly 2 years and 7 months. The 2008-2009 bear market lasted roughly 1 year and 4 months.

Let's say that the stock market peaks and then falls for more than 1 year. Further, there is plenty of pessimism on TV, in the newspapers and on the internet, and all of your friends are selling their stocks.

That is the time you want to be loading up on businesses like Coke, especially if it has fallen over 40% from its peak, has a P/E of 15 or less, and has a dividend yield approaching or exceeding 4%.

A time like this will come again. I do not know if it will happen in 2016, 2017, or later, but it is certain to come. Not even the Fed can stop it from happening.

So you want to be ready when this opportunity arrives.

It is July 2016 as I write this. The stock market has gone straight up since March 2009. We have had more than 7 years of a strong bull market, leaving stock valuations (P/E's) high and investors complacent.

Now is the time, in Buffett's words, to be fearful while others are being greedy.

If you raise your cash levels now, you will be ready.

You will have the cash available to buy great businesses like Coke during the next bear market.

Chapter 7: How to Get Started Today Investing like Warren Buffett

back to top

We've covered a lot of ground in this book. I hope that you are ready to take this information and use it to make money for yourself, investing in great businesses and great stocks.

Be sure to consult your financial advisor and tax advisor first, and if all looks good, just get started.

The best way to learn about investing is to start doing it. Start with very small positions, and then slowly increase them as your capital (and your confidence!) increases.

There's no better way to learn than simply by doing.

And I'm here to help you on your journey.

If you have questions, or just want to say hi, write to me at matt@trader.university

I love to hear from my readers, and I answer every email personally.

I hope that you will find investing "the Warren Buffett way" to be as rewarding as I have.

Before you go, I'd like to say "thank you" for purchasing Invest like Warren Buffett and reading it all the way to the end.

If you enjoyed this book and found it useful, I'd be very grateful if you'd post an honest review on Amazon. All you need to do is to <u>click here</u> and then click on the correct book cover.

Then click the blue link next to the yellow stars that says "customer reviews." You'll then see a gray button that says "Write a customer review"—click that and you're good to go.

If you would like to learn more ways to make money in the markets, check out my other Kindle books on the next page.

Keep Learning With These Trading Books

back to top

Rocket Stocks: Learn to Profit from the Stock Market's Biggest Winners

Monthly Cash Machine:Powerful Strategies for Selling Options in Bull and Bear Markets

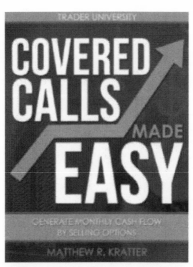

Covered Calls Made Easy
The Amazon #1 Bestseller for Options Trading

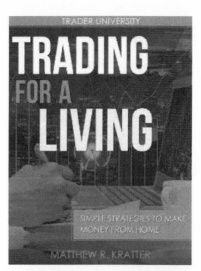

Trading For A Living

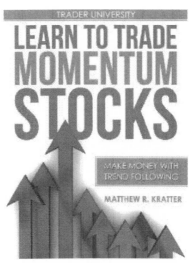

Learn to Trade Momentum Stocks

Rubber Band Stocks: A Simple Strategy for Trading Stocks

Your Free Gift

Thanks for purchasing my book!

As a way of showing my appreciation, I've created a "List of 24 Warren Buffett Stocks" for you.

After my book's initial publication, many of my readers asked for help finding the kind of great stocks that we discuss in this book.

So I put together a list of great businesses that are publicly traded. These are the kinds of stocks that Buffett already owns, or would probably own if he were investing smaller amounts of money, or if the price were right.

Download this list of stocks, and add them to your shopping list, so that you will be ready when the stock market sells off.

Simply go here to download your free list:

http://www.trader.university/buffett-bonus

About the Author

back to top

Hi there!

My name is Matthew Kratter. I am the founder of Trader University, and the best-selling author of multiple books on trading and investing. I have more than 20 years of trading experience, including working at multiple hedge funds.

Most individual traders and investors are at a huge disadvantage when it comes to the markets. Most are unable to invest in hedge funds. Yet, when they trade their own money, they are competing against computer algorithms, math PhD's, and multi-billion dollar hedge funds. I've been on the inside of many hedge funds. I know how professional traders and investors think and approach the markets. And I am committed to sharing their trading strategies with you in my books and courses.

When I am not trading or writing new books, I enjoy bodysurfing and otherwise hanging out at the beach with my wife, kids, and labradoodle.

If you enjoyed this book, you might also enjoy my other Kindle titles, which are available here:

www.Trader-Books.com

Or send me an email at matt@trader.university. I would love to hear from you.

Disclaimer

back to top

While the author has used his best efforts in preparing this book, he makes no representations or warranties with respect to the accuracy or completeness of the contents of this book and specifically disclaims any implied warranties or merchantability or fitness for a particular purpose. The advice and strategies contained herein may not be suitable for your situation. You should consult with a legal, financial, tax, or other professional where appropriate. Neither the publisher nor the author shall be liable for any loss of profit or any other commercial damages, including but not limited to special, incidental, consequential, or other damages.

This book is for educational purposes only. The views expressed are those of the author alone, and should not be taken as expert instruction or commands. The reader is responsible for his or her own actions.

Adherence to all applicable laws and regulations, including international, federal, state, and local laws, is the sole responsibility of the purchaser or reader.

Neither the author nor the publisher assumes any responsibility or liability whatsoever on the behalf of the purchaser or reader of these materials.

Any perceived slight of any individual or organization is purely unintentional.

Past performance is not necessarily indicative of future performance. Forex, futures, stock, and options trading is not appropriate for everyone. There is a substantial risk of loss associated with trading these markets. Losses can and will occur. No system or methodology has ever been developed that can guarantee profits or ensure freedom from losses. Nor will it likely ever be. No representation or implication is being made that using the methodologies or systems or the information contained within this book will generate profits or ensure freedom from losses. The information contained in this book is for educational purposes only and should NOT be taken as investment advice. Examples presented here are not solicitations to buy or sell. The author, publisher, and all affiliates assume no responsibility for your trading results. There is a high risk in trading.